Slow Cooker

Amazing meals with minimum effort

Linda Doeser

This edition published in 2009
Love Food ® is an imprint of Parragon Books Ltd

Parragon
Queen Street House
4 Queen Street
Bath BA1 1HE, UK

ISBN: 978-1-4075-7438-7

Printed in Indonesia

Author: Linda Doeser
Editor: Fiona Biggs
Designed by Fiona Roberts
Photography: Karen Thomas
Home Economist: Valerie Berry

Notes for the Reader

This book uses both metric and imperial measurements. Follow the same units of
measurement throughout; do not mix metric and imperial. All spoon measurements are level:
teaspoons are assumed to be 5 ml, and tablespoons are assumed to be 15 ml. Unless
otherwise stated, milk is assumed to be full fat, eggs and individual vegetables are medium,
and pepper is freshly ground black pepper.

The times given are an approximate guide only. Preparation times differ according to the
techniques used by different people and the cooking times may also vary from those given.
Optional ingredients, variations or serving suggestions have not been included in the
calculations.

Recipes using raw or very lightly cooked eggs should be avoided by infants, the elderly,
pregnant women, convalescents and anyone suffering from an illness. Pregnant and
breastfeeding women are advised to avoid eating peanuts and peanut products. Sufferers
from nut allergies should be aware that some of the ready-made ingredients used in the
recipes in this book may contain nuts. Always check the packaging before use.

Contents

INTRODUCTION

Slow cooking is not a new concept. There are hundreds of traditional slow-cooked dishes from all around the world, ranging from Tuscan stufato to Boston baked beans.

All kinds of containers have been contrived for just this purpose over the centuries, from the Maori hangi, an earth pit used to cook fabulous feasts, to the hay box, beloved of a generation of boy scouts. The electric slow cooker first appeared in the United States and Europe some thirty years ago and was intended to make this delicious method of cooking easier, more convenient and less expensive.

The designers of today's new generation of slow cookers have developed and improved the original idea with the needs and demands of a twenty-first-century lifestyle in mind. There are so many conflicting calls on our time that preparing home-cooked meals has become increasingly difficult. It's not even always possible to know what time you and the rest of the family are going to get home. The slow cooker provides a healthier and more economical solution than ready-cooked meals or home deliveries, combined with all the flavour of freshly cooked food. Of course, you do have to spend a little time in the kitchen preparing ingredients, but once everything is in the pot, you can safely leave it to cook while you get on with the rest of your life. Because the slow cooker cooks at a low temperature for a long time, you don't have to worry about pans boiling dry and food being spoiled if you're slightly delayed.

The slow cooker is also invaluable when you are entertaining. You can arrange your preparation time more conveniently so that, for example, you can concentrate on decorating an elaborate dessert while the main course is quietly simmering to perfection. It is also useful at that tricky moment when your guests arrive and you want to chat, as you don't have to worry about what is happening in the kitchen. For more informal gatherings, the slow cooker is ideal for preparing hot snacks and great for rounding off an evening at the cinema or theatre with a late night supper.

Although it's wonderful to come home on a cold winter's evening to a welcoming pot of goulash or curry, the slow cooker is just as useful in the summer when the last thing you want to do is slave over a hot stove but the family has grown bored with endless plates of salad. In fact, in some ways, it's even more useful in the summer as it gives out very little heat while it's cooking so the kitchen remains cool and pleasant.

What's cooking?

Almost all kinds of foods can be cooked in a slow cooker. Hearty casseroles, stews and soups remain the most popular choices, but you can also prepare starters, desserts, delicate items like fish, snacks, side dishes, small joints of meat and even hot punch or a wine cup for a party.

Slow cooking is the ideal way to prepare less expensive, less tender cuts of meat, such as braising steak and chicken thighs, as these benefit from prolonged cooking.

However, not every dish takes a whole day to cook. Some can be timed perfectly to be ready for lunch when you return from a morning's shopping or to provide an after-match snack on a Saturday afternoon.

The slow cooker is not just for meat-eaters. Vegetarian main courses and vegetable accompaniments can also be cooked this way. However, root vegetables in particular take a surprisingly long time – often longer than meat. It is the ideal method for cooking pulses as you need have no worries about a pan boiling over or boiling dry.

In fact, there is very little that can't be cooked in a slow cooker. Pasta is a notable exception as it needs to be boiled quite vigorously rather than gently simmered. This doesn't really present a problem as it cooks so rapidly in a conventional saucepan. However, if you do want to add pasta to a dish in the slow cooker, boil it first until it is nearly tender, then add it to the cooker for the last 20–30 minutes of the cooking time. Rice is somewhat similar. Again, as it cooks quite quickly, it makes an easy accompaniment. For dishes where rice is an integral part, such as paella or jambalaya, it's best to add cooked rather than raw rice for the last 30 minutes of cooking time.

Ingredients with a delicate texture cannot withstand prolonged cooking. Fish and seafood, for example, will fall apart, so they are best added shortly before the end of cooking. Fish, raw seafood and live shellfish take 30–60 minutes in a slow cooker, while cooked prawns take 15–30

minutes. In both cases, they should be cooked on the high setting. It's best to add mushrooms towards the end of the cooking time.

Types of cooker

A cooker with a 4.5-litre/8-pint working capacity is ideal for most families. An oval cooker offers more flexibility than a round one as it can more easily accommodate small joints of meat, such as lamb shanks, or a whole fish.

Modern slow cookers usually have a removable ceramic cooking pot but in older models the cooking container was often fixed inside the outer casing, making them more awkward to wash as the base unit must never be immersed in water. The lids on modern models and some older ones are usually made of heatproof glass. This allows you to monitor progress without uncovering the food, which would lower the temperature.

The base unit is made of metal and may be encased in a heatproof material. Two or more feet ensure stability. The handles are also usually made from a cool-touch material.

The controls on modern cookers are usually in the form of a dial and may include several settings – typically, high, low and auto, and some also include medium. There will also be an off position. There may be a light to indicate when the cooker is switched on. However, not all older cookers have an off position and must be switched off at the mains socket. They do have a high and low setting.

It is essential to read the manufacturer's instructions carefully before using the cooker for the first time. These will explain the settings and safety features, as well as describing the methods for cleaning and general care of the cooker.

Using the slow cooker

Place the cooker on a level worktop, ensuring that the cord does not overhang the edge. Check that the control switch is in the off position before you plug the cooker into the mains.

If your cooker has a removable cooking pot, lift it out of the base unit when placing the ingredients in it to avoid spills and splashes which can damage the base unit. For the same reason, you should not fill the cooking pot more than about two-thirds full. When you're ready to use the cooker put the cooking pot back into position, fit the lid and switch on. Do not switch the base unit on without the cooking pot in position. Never put food or liquid directly into the base unit.

Modern slow cookers work by building up the heat and then maintaining an even temperature. Some older cookers must be preheated (see the manufacturer's instructions). As the food cooks, liquid evaporates and condenses on the lid, forming a seal. You should not lift the lid off the cooker for at least the first half of the cooking time. Very often, it will not be necessary to raise the lid until you're ready to serve. Food cooked in a slow cooker rarely needs stirring.

When the cooker is on the low setting it is safe to leave it unattended. The high setting cooks about twice as fast as the low one and manufacturers recommend that you keep an eye on the food while it is cooking. If you want to cook on high and need to go out or you're cooking overnight, it is best to use the auto setting, if your slow cooker has one, because the cooker starts cooking on high and then switches to low.

When the food is cooked, switch the dial to the off position and unplug the cooker. Handle the cooking pot with oven gloves as it will be very hot. Let the base unit and the cooking pot cool completely before you clean them. The pot and lid should be washed in warm soapy water, rinsed and dried, or washed in the dishwasher if suitable. The base unit usually requires nothing more than wiping with a soft, dry cloth. Do not immerse the base unit in water.

Preparing food

In general, ingredients can be prepared for cooking in a slow cooker in very much the same way as they are for cooking in the oven or on the hob. However, there are a few guidelines which are worth following.

Trim any visible fat from meat. You can also skim off excess grease with a skimmer or spoon after cooking. Meat and poultry look more attractive and retain more flavour if they are seared first. Cook in a little oil over a medium heat, stirring and turning occasionally, until browned on all sides. This also helps to reduce fat as you can pour it off from the pan or drain the meat with a slotted spoon.

Cut root vegetables into small pieces, precook them for 5 minutes in a little oil and place them in the base of the cooker to ensure that they are immersed in liquid.

Most dried pulses need to be soaked before cooking and some must be boiled vigorously for 15 minutes to destroy naturally occurring toxins. These include aduki, black, black-eyed, borlotti and red kidney beans. Bring them to the boil in a saucepan, boil rapidly for 15 minutes, then drain and rinse before cooking in the slow cooker. Soya beans require pre-boiling for 1 hour because they contain a substance that prevents the body from absorbing protein.

As there is less evaporation in the slow cooker than with conventional cooking, less liquid is required. However, some liquid is essential. To reach the optimum temperature as quickly as possible – essential for food safety – bring the liquid to the boil before adding it to the cooker. If the sauce is too thin, stir a little cornflour (1–2 tablespoons) to a paste with some water, then stir it into the cooker. Turn the control switch to high and cook for a further 15 minutes.

Dairy products are best added about 30 minutes before serving to avoid curdling.

Hints and tips

◎ Position the cooker out of the reach of children and make sure that the electric cable does not hang down from the work surface.

◎ Don't lift the lid and poke the food with a spoon during cooking as this will cause a rapid drop in temperature.

◎ The cooking times given in the recipes are guidelines but many factors can affect them. Older pulses, for example, take longer to cook than more recently harvested ones.

◎ Hot steam will rise out of the cooker when you remove the lid so don't peer into it and risk scalding your face.

◎ Use oven gloves when you lift out the cooking pot at the end of cooking and place a mat underneath the pot.

◎ Check that food is cooked through. This is especially important with poultry for health reasons. Pierce the thickest part – if the juices run clear, it is cooked through.

◎ Don't put the pot down on a hot hob, and when you've finished don't put the lid in cold water.

◎ Don't use the slow cooker if any of it is damaged, including the cable and plug. A chip in the cooking pot makes a great breeding site for bacteria.

◎ Don't leave leftovers in the cooking pot. Reheat them in the oven or on the hob, not in the slow cooker.

◎ Don't use the slow cooker for thawing frozen food as this can be a health hazard.

◎ Make sure the cooking pot is dry before re-using it.

◎ Only fill the cooking pot about two-thirds full to allow room for expansion during cooking.

◎ If food has stuck to the cooking pot, fill it with warm soapy water and leave to soak. Don't use scouring pads or abrasives to clean the pot as these will scratch it and food will stick to the scratches next time you use it.

1

CHAPTER 1: SIMPLE STARTERS AND SNACKS

GREEK BEAN & VEGETABLE SOUP

*A great first course, this colourful country soup also makes a delicious
light lunch served with Greek poppy seed bread.*

Serves 4–6

Preparation time: 15 minutes, plus overnight soaking

Cooking time: 12 hours

Ingredients

500g/1 lb 2 oz dried haricot beans,
  soaked in cold water overnight

2 onions, finely chopped

2 garlic cloves, finely chopped

2 potatoes, chopped

2 carrots, chopped

2 tomatoes, peeled and chopped

2 celery sticks, chopped

4 tbsp extra virgin olive oil

1 bay leaf

salt and pepper

To garnish

12 black olives

2 tbsp chopped fresh chives

1 Drain the beans and rinse well under cold running water. Place them in the slow cooker and add the
onions, garlic, potatoes, carrots, tomatoes, celery, olive oil and bay leaf.

2 Pour in 2 litres/3½ pints boiling water, making sure that all the ingredients are fully submerged.
Cover and cook on low for 12 hours until the beans are tender.

3 Remove and discard the bay leaf. Season the soup to taste with salt and pepper and stir in the olives
and chives. Ladle into warm soup bowls and serve.

Cook's tip
*Haricot beans do not need to be vigorously boiled
for 15 minutes at the beginning of cooking.*

Variation
*For a more substantial soup, add a meaty ham bone with
all the other ingredients in step 1. Before serving, remove
the bone, cut off the meat and return it to the soup.*

COCK-A-LEEKIE

This is a two-for-the-price-of-one dish as you can serve the broth
as a first course and serve the chicken for the main course.

Serves 6–8

Preparation time: 15 minutes, plus 7 hours' soaking

Cooking time: 7½ hours

Ingredients

12 prunes, stoned, or 12 ready-to-eat prunes

4 chicken portions

450 g/1 lb leeks, sliced

1.4 litres/2½ pints hot chicken or beef stock

1 bouquet garni

salt and pepper

1 If using ordinary prunes, place them in a bowl and add cold water to cover. Set aside to soak while the soup is cooking.

2 Place the chicken portions and leeks in the slow cooker. Pour in the stock and add the bouquet garni. Cover and cook on low for 7 hours.

3 If you are going to serve the chicken with the soup, remove it from the cooker with a slotted spoon and cut the meat off the bones. Cut it into bite-sized pieces and return it to the cooker. Otherwise, leave the chicken portions in the slow cooker.

4 Drain the prunes, if necessary. Add the prunes to the soup and season to taste with salt and pepper. Re-cover and cook on high for 30 minutes.

5 Remove and discard the bouquet garni. Either ladle the soup, including the cut-up chicken, into warm bowls or remove the chicken portions and keep warm for the main course, then ladle the broth into warm bowls. Serve immediately.

Cook's tip
Home-made stock is always best, but you can use good-quality stock cubes or bouillon powder. Be careful when seasoning the soup as stock cubes may be extra salty.

Variation
In the traditional Scottish recipe a piece of beef was cooked with the chicken. You can replace half the chicken with 550 g/1 lb 4 oz stewing beef in a single piece. Tie it with string to keep it in shape. Cut it into pieces with the chicken and return to the soup.

TEX-MEX BEAN DIP

Not only is this spicy warm dip a tasty starter, but it is also an ideal party snack. Serve it with a selection of dippers if you like.

Serves 4

Preparation time: 15 minutes, plus 5 minutes' pre-cooking

Cooking time: 2 hours

Ingredients

2 tbsp corn oil

1 onion, finely chopped

2 garlic cloves, finely chopped

2–3 fresh green chillies, deseeded
    and finely chopped

400 g/14 oz canned refried beans
    or red kidney beans

2 tbsp chilli sauce or taco sauce

6 tbsp hot vegetable stock

115 g/4 oz Cheddar cheese, grated

salt and pepper

1 fresh red chilli, deseeded and
    shredded, to garnish

tortilla chips, to serve

1 Heat the oil in a large, heavy-based frying pan. Add the onion, garlic and chillies and cook, stirring occasionally, over a low heat for 5 minutes until the onion is soft and translucent. Transfer to the slow cooker.

2 Add the refried beans to the slow cooker. If using red kidney beans, drain well and rinse under cold running water. Reserve 2 tablespoons of the beans and mash the remainder coarsely with a potato masher. Add all the beans to the slow cooker.

3 Add the sauce, hot stock and grated cheese, season with salt and pepper and stir well. Cover and cook on low for 2 hours.

4 Transfer the dip to a serving bowl, garnish with shredded red chilli and serve warm with tortilla chips on the side.

Cook's tip
*Chillies vary considerably in their degree of hotness.
As a general rule, small pointed chillies tend to be
hotter than larger blunt ones, but even pods from
the same plant can vary.*

LOUISIANA COURGETTES

An attractive vegetarian starter, this lightly spiced dish can also be served as an accompaniment to chicken or simply grilled fish.

Serves 6

Preparation time: 15 minutes

Cooking time: 2½ hours

Ingredients

1 kg/2 lb 4 oz courgettes, thickly sliced

1 onion, finely chopped

2 garlic cloves, finely chopped

2 red peppers, deseeded and chopped

5 tbsp hot vegetable stock

4 tomatoes, peeled and chopped

25 g/1 oz butter, diced

salt and cayenne pepper

3 tbsp chopped fresh parsley, to garnish

1 Place the courgettes, onion, garlic and red peppers in the slow cooker and season to taste with salt and cayenne pepper. Pour in the stock and mix well.

2 Sprinkle the chopped tomato on top and dot with the butter. Cover and cook on high for 2½ hours until tender. Garnish with the parsley and serve.

Cook's tip
To peel tomatoes, score a cross in the bottom end and place in a heatproof bowl. Pour in boiling water to cover and leave to stand for 30–60 seconds. Drain and refresh under cold water. The skins will then peel away easily.

Variation
Replace half the courgettes with patty pan squash and substitute a mixture of 4 tablespoons uncoloured dry breadcrumbs and 4 tablespoons grated Parmesan cheese for the tomatoes. Cover and cook on low for 6 hours.

SWEET-AND-SOUR CHICKEN WINGS

Messy but delicious, chicken wings are also good to serve as party nibbles – just increase the quantity.

Serves 4–6

Preparation time: 10 minutes, plus 10 minutes for the sauce

Cooking time: 5 hours

Ingredients

1 kg/1 lb 4 oz chicken wings, tips removed

2 celery sticks, chopped

700 ml/1¼ pints hot chicken stock

2 tbsp cornflour

3 tbsp white wine vinegar or rice vinegar

3 tbsp dark soy sauce

5 tbsp sweet chilli sauce

55 g/2 oz soft brown sugar

400 g/14 oz canned pineapple
　chunks in juice, drained

200 g/7 oz canned sliced bamboo
　shoots, drained and rinsed

½ green pepper, deseeded and thinly sliced

½ red pepper, deseeded and thinly sliced

salt

1 Put the chicken wings and celery in the slow cooker and season with salt. Pour in the chicken stock, cover and cook on low for 5 hours.

2 Drain the chicken wings, reserving 350 ml/12 fl oz of the stock, and keep warm. Pour the reserved stock into a saucepan and stir in the cornflour. Add the vinegar, soy sauce and chilli sauce. Place over a medium heat and stir in the sugar. Cook, stirring constantly, for 5 minutes, or until the sugar has dissolved completely and the sauce is thickened, smooth and clear.

3 Lower the heat, stir in the pineapple, bamboo shoots and peppers and simmer gently for 2–3 minutes. Stir in the chicken wings until they are thoroughly coated, then transfer to a serving platter.

Variation
You can add other flavourings to the sauce if you like, but make sure that they are all very thinly sliced so that they cook quickly. Try strips of carrot and fresh root ginger.

CHAPTER 2: EVERYDAY MEALS

TRADITIONAL POT ROAST

*There is something almost magical about coming home on a cold day
to a tender beef pot roast and all its accompanying vegetables.*

🍽 Serves 6
🥣 Preparation time: 20 minutes
🍳 Cooking time: 9–10 hours

Ingredients

1 onion, finely chopped

4 carrots, sliced

4 baby turnips sliced

4 celery sticks, sliced

2 potatoes, peeled and sliced

1 sweet potato, peeled and sliced

1.3–1.8 kg/3–4 lb topside of beef

1 bouquet garni

300 ml/10 fl oz hot beef stock

salt and pepper

1 Place the onion, carrots, turnips, celery, potatoes and sweet potato in the slow cooker and stir to
mix well.

2 Rub the beef all over with salt and pepper, then place on top of the bed of vegetables. Add the
bouquet garni and pour in the stock. Cover and cook on low for 9–10 hours, until the beef is cooked
to your liking.

3 Remove the beef, carve into slices and arrange on serving plates. Spoon some of the vegetables
and cooking juices onto the plates and serve.

Cook's tip
*If you like thickened gravy, keep the meat and vegetables
warm, transfer the cooking juices to a small saucepan and
place over a low heat. Stir 1 tablespoon cornflour with 2
tablespoons water to make a paste, stir into the cooking
juices and bring to the boil, stirring constantly, until thick.*

Variation
*You can add or substitute all kinds of vegetables to this
traditional, but basic recipe. For example, you could
substitute 2 sliced leeks for the onion and swede for the
turnips. You could also replace half the beef stock with
red wine, if you like.*

BRUNSWICK STEW

*Nothing is nicer on a cold winter's evening than sitting down
to this hearty traditional American one-pot dish.*

Serves 4

Preparation time: 20 minutes, plus 10 minutes' pre-cooking

Cooking time: 7 hours

Ingredients

3 tbsp corn oil

1 large onion, thinly sliced

1 green pepper, deseeded and chopped

8 chicken pieces, such as thighs and drumsticks

400 g/14 oz canned chopped tomatoes,
  drained

pinch of cayenne pepper

1 tbsp Worcestershire sauce

300 ml/10 fl oz hot chicken stock

1 tbsp cornflour

200 g/7 oz frozen sweetcorn, thawed

450 g/1 lb frozen broad beans, thawed

salt

crusty bread, to serve

1 Heat the oil in a large, heavy-based frying pan. Add the onion and pepper and cook over a medium heat, stirring occasionally, for 5 minutes until the onion is softened. Using a slotted spoon, transfer the mixture to the slow cooker.

2 Add the chicken to the pan and cook, turning occasionally, for 5 minutes until golden all over. Transfer to the slow cooker and add the tomatoes. Season with a pinch of cayenne pepper and salt. Stir the Worcestershire sauce into the hot stock and pour into the slow cooker. Cover and cook on low for 6½ hours.

3 Mix the cornflour to a paste with 2–3 tablespoons water and stir into the stew. Add the sweetcorn and beans, re-cover and cook on high for 30–40 minutes until everything is cooked through and piping hot. Transfer to warm plates and serve with crusty bread.

Variation
*If you like, you can use canned sweetcorn
and broad beans. Drain well and rinse
under cold water, then drain again.*

NUTTY CHICKEN

*Chicken simmers to tender perfection in a rich sauce flavoured
with walnuts, lemon, ginger and, surprisingly, black treacle.*

Serves 4

Preparation time: 15 minutes, plus 10–15 minutes' pre-cooking

Cooking time: 6 hours

Ingredients

3 tbsp sunflower oil

4 skinless chicken portions

2 shallots, chopped

1 tsp ground ginger

1 tbsp plain flour

425 ml/15 fl oz beef stock

55 g/2 oz walnut pieces

grated rind of 1 lemon

2 tbsp lemon juice

1 tbsp black treacle

salt and pepper

fresh watercress sprigs, to garnish

1 Heat the oil in a large, heavy-based frying pan. Season the chicken portions with salt and pepper and
add to the pan. Cook over a medium heat, turning occasionally, for 5–8 minutes, until lightly golden all
over. Transfer to the slow cooker.

2 Add the shallots to the pan and cook, stirring occasionally, for 3–4 minutes until softened. Sprinkle in
the ginger and flour and cook, stirring constantly, for 1 minute. Gradually stir in the stock and bring to the
boil, stirring constantly. Lower the heat and simmer for 1 minute, then stir in the nuts, lemon rind and juice
and treacle.

3 Pour the sauce over the chicken. Cover and cook on low for 6 hours until the chicken is cooked through
and tender. Taste and adjust the seasoning if necessary. Transfer the chicken to warm plates, spoon some
of the sauce over each portion, garnish with watercress sprigs and serve immediately.

Variation
*If you prefer you can use pecans instead of
walnuts and molasses instead of black treacle.*

GOULASH

There are many versions of this traditional beef stew, which dates back to the ninth century. Finishing it with soured cream is, however, a modern addition.

Serves 4

Preparation time: 20 minutes, plus 25 minutes' pre-cooking

Cooking time: 9 hours

Ingredients

4 tbsp sunflower oil

650 g/1 lb 7 oz braising steak, cut
    into 2.5-cm/1-in cubes

2 tsp plain flour

2 tsp paprika

300 ml/10 fl oz beef stock

3 onions, chopped

4 carrots, diced

1 large potato or 2 medium potatoes, diced

1 bay leaf

½–1 tsp caraway seeds

400 g/14 oz canned chopped tomatoes

2 tbsp soured cream

salt and pepper

1 Heat half the oil in a heavy-based frying pan. Add the beef and cook over a medium heat, stirring frequently, until browned all over. Lower the heat and stir in the flour and paprika. Cook, stirring constantly, for 2 minutes. Gradually stir in the stock and bring to the boil, then transfer the mixture to the slow cooker.

2 Rinse out the frying pan and heat the remaining oil in it. Add the onions and cook over a low heat, stirring occasionally, for 5 minutes until softened. Stir in the carrots and potato and cook for a few minutes more. Add the bay leaf, caraway seeds and tomatoes with their can juices. Season with salt and pepper.

3 Transfer the vegetable mixture to the slow cooker, stir well, then cover and cook on low for 9 hours until the meat is tender.

4 Remove and discard the bay leaf. Stir in the soured cream and serve immediately.

Cook's tip
*Use sweet Hungarian paprika for the best flavour.
Caraway seeds have a highly distinctive taste a
little like aniseed, so you may want to adjust the
quantity or even omit them altogether.*

MEXICAN PORK CHOPS

Pork is traditionally served with sharp-flavoured fruit to counterbalance its richness.
This unusual and refreshing recipe uses pineapple to do this.

Serves 4

Preparation time: 15 minutes, plus 10 minutes' pre-cooking

Cooking time: 6¼ hours

Ingredients

4 pork chops, trimmed of excess fat

2 tbsp corn oil

450 g/1 lb canned pineapple cubes in fruit juice

1 red pepper, deseeded and finely chopped

2 fresh jalapeño chillies, deseeded and
   finely chopped

1 onion, finely chopped

1 tbsp chopped fresh coriander

125 ml/4 fl oz hot chicken stock

salt and pepper

fresh coriander sprigs, to garnish

1 Season the chops with salt and pepper. Heat the oil in a large, heavy-based frying pan. Add the chops and cook over a medium heat for 2–3 minutes each side until lightly browned. Transfer them to the slow cooker. Drain the pineapple, reserving the juice, and set aside.

2 Add the red pepper, chillies and onion to the frying pan and cook, stirring occasionally, for 5 minutes until the onion is softened. Transfer the mixture to the slow cooker and add the coriander and stock, together with 125 ml/4 fl oz of the reserved pineapple juice. Cover and cook on low for 6 hours until the chops are tender.

3 Add the reserved pineapple to the slow cooker, re-cover and cook on high for 15 minutes. Serve immediately, garnished with fresh coriander sprigs.

Cook's tip
Jalapeño chillies are the best-known Mexican chillies and may be green or red. They are quite small, blunt and fleshy, with a medium hot flavour.

Variation
You could substitute 650 g/1 lb 7 oz cubed boneless shoulder of pork for the chops and canned mandarin oranges for the pineapple.

GAMMON COOKED IN CIDER

This is a great way to cook a gammon joint as it prevents the meat from drying out and allows the delicious spicy flavours to penetrate.

Serves 6

Preparation time: 10 minutes, plus 15 minutes' standing

Cooking time: 8 hours

Ingredients

1 kg/2 lb 4 oz boneless gammon joint

1 onion, halved

4 cloves

6 black peppercorns

1 tsp juniper berries

1 celery stick, chopped

1 carrot, sliced

1 litre/1¾ pints medium cider

fresh vegetables, such as mashed
    potatoes and peas, to serve

1 Place a trivet or rack in the slow cooker, if you like, and stand the gammon on it. Otherwise, just place the gammon in the cooker. Stud each of the onion halves with 2 cloves and add to the cooker with the peppercorns, juniper berries, celery and carrot.

2 Pour in the cider, cover and cook on low for 8 hours until the meat is tender.

3 Remove the gammon from the cooker and place on a board. Tent with foil and leave to stand for 10–15 minutes. Discard the cooking liquid and flavourings.

4 Cut off any rind and fat from the gammon joint, then carve into slices and serve with fresh vegetables.

Cook's tip
However joints of meat are cooked, including in the slow cooker, they benefit from being allowed to stand before carving. This evens up the texture of the meat so it is easier to carve into neat slices. Loosely covering the gammon with foil keeps it hot.

POOR MAN'S CASSOULET

This is an inexpensive and easy version of a much more elaborate and time-consuming French dish – but it's very good on a cold evening.

 Serves 4

 Preparation time: 10 minutes, plus 10 minutes' pre-cooking

 Cooking time: 6 hours

Ingredients

2 tbsp sunflower oil

2 onions, chopped

2 garlic cloves, finely chopped

115 g/4 oz streaky bacon,
  derinded and chopped

500 g/1 lb 2 oz pork sausages

400 g/14 oz canned haricot, red kidney or
  black-eyed beans, drained and rinsed

2 tbsp chopped fresh parsley

150 ml/5 fl oz hot beef stock

To serve

4 slices French bread

55 g/2 oz Gruyère cheese, grated

1 Heat the oil in a heavy-based frying pan. Add the onions and cook over a low heat, stirring occasionally, for 5 minutes until softened. Add the garlic, bacon and sausages and cook, stirring and turning the sausages occasionally, for a further 5 minutes.

2 Using a slotted spoon, transfer the mixture from the frying pan to the slow cooker. Add the beans, parsley and beef stock, then cover and cook on low for 6 hours.

3 Just before serving, lightly toast the bread under a preheated grill. Divide the grated cheese among the toast slices and place under the grill until just melted.

4 Ladle the cassoulet onto warm plates, top each portion with the cheese-toast and serve.

Cook's tip
For the best results, use top-quality sausages, or chipolatas if you prefer, and for a special occasion, splash out on wild boar or venison sausages.

PORK WITH ALMONDS

Olives, chillies, capers and, of course, almonds provide a delicious mix of flavours in this traditional Mexican stew.

Serves 4

Preparation time: 25 minutes, plus 25 minutes' pre-cooking

Cooking time: 5 hours

Ingredients

2 tbsp corn or sunflower oil

2 onions, chopped

2 garlic cloves, finely chopped

5-cm/2-inch cinnamon stick

3 cloves

115 g/4 oz ground almonds

750 g/1 lb 10 oz boneless pork,
    cut into 2.5-cm/1-inch cubes

4 tomatoes, peeled and chopped

2 tbsp capers

115 g/4 oz green olives, stoned

3 pickled jalapeño chillies, drained,
    deseeded and cut into rings

350 ml/12 fl oz chicken stock

salt and pepper

fresh coriander sprigs,
    to garnish (optional)

1 Heat half the oil in a large, heavy-based frying pan. Add the onions and cook over a low heat, stirring occasionally, for 5 minutes until softened. Add the garlic, cinnamon, cloves and almonds and cook, stirring frequently, for 8–10 minutes. Be careful not to burn the almonds.

2 Remove and discard the spices and transfer the mixture to a food processor. Process to a smooth purée.

3 Rinse out the pan and return to the heat. Heat the remaining oil, then add the pork, in batches if necessary. Cook over a medium heat, stirring frequently, for 5–10 minutes until browned all over. Return all the pork to the pan and add the almond purée, tomatoes, capers, olives, chillies and chicken stock. Bring to the boil, then transfer to the slow cooker.

4 Season with salt and pepper and mix well. Cover and cook on low for 5 hours. To serve, transfer to warm plates and garnish with coriander sprigs, if desired.

Cook's tip
The small flower buds from the caper bush are sold preserved in a mixture of salt and vinegar or in salt alone. Pickled capers need to be rinsed, but those preserved in salt alone can simply be brushed with your fingertips.

TAGLIATELLE WITH PRAWNS

*This lovely summery dish is perfect for family suppers
and is special enough to serve to guests.*

 Serves 4
 Preparation time: 5 minutes
 Cooking time: 7¼ hours

Ingredients

400 g/14 oz tomatoes, peeled
  and chopped
140 g/5 oz tomato purée
1 garlic clove, finely chopped
2 tbsp chopped fresh parsley
500 g/1 lb 2 oz cooked, peeled
  Mediterranean prawns

6 fresh basil leaves, torn
400 g/14 oz dried tagliatelle
salt and pepper
fresh basil leaves, to garnish

1 Put the tomatoes, tomato purée, garlic and parsley in the slow cooker and season with salt and pepper.
Cover and cook on low for 7 hours.

2 Add the prawns and basil. Re-cover and cook on high for 15 minutes.

3 Meanwhile, bring a large saucepan of lightly salted water to the boil. Add the pasta, bring back to the
boil and cook for 10–12 minutes until tender but still firm to the bite.

4 Drain the pasta and tip it into a warm serving bowl. Add the prawn sauce and toss lightly with 2 large
forks. Garnish with the basil leaves and serve immediately.

Cook's tip
*For the richest flavour, use sun-ripened tomatoes.
Those ripened under glass lack sweetness and tend
to be watery. If they're all that's available, you can
substitute canned chopped tomatoes instead.*

Variation
*Substitute 425 g/15 oz drained, canned clams
for the prawns for tagliatelle alle vongole.*

VEGETABLE HOTPOT WITH PARSLEY DUMPLINGS

This hearty, one-pot, vegetarian dish is simplicity itself, but if you're too tired to bother with the dumplings, just serve it with fresh crusty bread.

 Serves 6

 Preparation time: 20 minutes

 Cooking time: 6½ hours

Ingredients

½ swede, cut into chunks

2 onions, sliced

2 potatoes, cut into chunks

2 carrots, cut into chunks

2 celery sticks, sliced

2 courgettes, sliced

2 tbsp tomato purée

600 ml/1 pint hot vegetable stock

1 bay leaf

1 tsp ground coriander

½ tsp dried thyme

400 g/14 oz canned sweetcorn, drained

salt and pepper

For the parsley dumplings

200 g/7 oz self-raising flour

115 g/4 oz vegetable suet

2 tbsp chopped fresh parsley

125 ml/4 fl oz milk

1 Put the swede, onions, potatoes, carrots, celery and courgettes into the slow cooker. Stir the tomato purée into the stock and pour it over the vegetables. Add the bay leaf, coriander and thyme and season with salt and pepper. Cover and cook on low for 6 hours.

2 To make the dumplings, sift the flour with a pinch of salt into a bowl and stir in the suet and parsley. Add just enough milk to make a firm but light dough. Knead lightly and shape into 12 small balls.

3 Stir the sweetcorn into the vegetable casserole and place the dumplings on top. Cook on high for 30 minutes. Serve immediately.

Cook's tip
It can be quite tricky to cook vegetables well in a slow cooker and they can often take longer than you think. It's important, therefore, to cut them into even chunks of about the same size.

Variation
You can substitute or add whatever vegetables you like best. For example, swap leeks for the onions, a sweet potato for the ordinary potatoes and fennel for the celery. If you like, substitute canned pulses, such as kidney beans or cannellini beans for the sweetcorn.

BOSTON BAKED BEANS

This traditional American dish can be served on its own with plenty of warm, fresh bread or as an accompaniment to roast pork.

Serves 4–6

Preparation time: 15 minutes, plus overnight soaking

Cooking time: 3 + 11 hours (14 hours in total)

Ingredients

450 g/1 lb dried white haricot beans, soaked
   overnight in cold water and drained
115 g/4 oz salt pork, soaked in cold
   water for 3 hours and drained
1 onion, chopped
3 tbsp molasses or black treacle
3 tbsp muscovado sugar
2 tsp dry mustard
salt and pepper

1 Place the beans in the slow cooker and add about
1.4 litres/2 $\frac{1}{2}$ pints boiling water so that they are
covered. Cover and cook on high for 3 hours.
Meanwhile, cut the salt pork into chunks.

2 Drain the beans, reserving 225 ml/8 fl oz of the
cooking liquid. Mix the reserved liquid with the
molasses, sugar, mustard and 1 teaspoon salt.

3 Return the beans to the slow cooker and add the
salt pork, onion and the molasses mixture. Stir, then
cover and cook on low for 11 hours.

4 Adjust the seasoning and serve immediately.

Cook's tip
*Molasses is a by-product when sugar cane is refined. It is
thick, dark and very concentrated with a distinctively rich
flavour. It is not so sweet as other syrups, and blackstrap
molasses, in particular, has quite a bitter taste.*

Variation
*This was never intended as a vegetarian dish, but you
could make a meatless version by omitting the salt pork
and stirring in 115 g/4 oz grated Cheddar cheese at
the end of cooking.*

WARM CHICKPEA SALAD

Chickpeas have a deliciously nutty flavour that works well with a herbed dressing.
They are notorious for taking ages to cook, so the slow cooker solves the problem.

Serves 6

Preparation time: 10 minutes

Cooking time: 12 hours

Ingredients

225 g/8 oz dried chickpeas, soaked
   overnight in cold water and drained

115 g/4 oz stoned black olives

4 spring onions, finely chopped

fresh parsley sprigs, to garnish

crusty bread, to serve

For the dressing

2 tbsp red wine vinegar

2 tbsp mixed chopped fresh herbs, such
   as parsley, rosemary and thyme

3 garlic cloves, very finely chopped

125 ml/4 fl oz extra virgin olive oil

salt and pepper

1 Place the chickpeas in the slow cooker and add sufficient boiling water to cover. Cover and cook on low for 12 hours.

2 Drain well and transfer to a bowl. Stir in the olives and spring onions.

3 To make the dressing, whisk together the vinegar, herbs and garlic in a jug and season with salt and pepper to taste. Gradually whisk in the olive oil. Pour the dressing over the still-warm chickpeas and toss lightly to coat. Garnish with the parsley sprigs and serve warm with crusty bread.

Cook's tip
This also makes a tasty starter for 8–10 people. You can
make it in advance and serve cold, but not chilled.

CHAPTER 3: LOW FAT

VEGETABLE CURRY

*This is a wonderfully adaptable recipe that can be served
with other Indian dishes or simply with plain boiled rice.*

Serves 4–6

Preparation time: 15 minutes, plus 20 minutes' pre-cooking

Cooking time: 5 hours

Ingredients

2 tbsp vegetable oil

1 tsp cumin seeds

1 onion, sliced

2 curry leaves

2.5-cm/1-in piece fresh root ginger, finely
    chopped

2 fresh red chillies, deseeded and chopped

2 tbsp curry paste

2 carrots, sliced

115 g/4 oz mangetouts

1 cauliflower, cut into florets

3 tomatoes, peeled and chopped

85 g/3 oz frozen peas, thawed

$\frac{1}{2}$ tsp turmeric

150–225 ml/5–8 fl oz hot vegetable
    or chicken stock

salt and pepper

1 Heat the oil in a large, heavy-based saucepan. Add the cumin seeds and cook, stirring constantly,
for 1–2 minutes until they give off their aroma and begin to pop. Add the onion and curry leaves and
cook, stirring occasionally, for 5 minutes until the onion has softened. Add the ginger and chillies
and cook, stirring occasionally, for 1 minute.

2 Stir in the curry paste and cook, stirring, for 2 minutes, then add the carrots, mangetouts and cauliflower
florets. Cook for 5 minutes, then add the tomatoes, peas and turmeric and season with salt and pepper.
Cook for 3 minutes, then add 150 ml/5 fl oz of the stock and bring to the boil.

3 Transfer the mixture to the slow cooker. If the vegetables are not covered, add more hot stock, then
cover and cook on low for 5 hours until tender. Remove and discard the curry leaves before serving.

Cook's tip
*Curry leaves are used in Indian cooking in the same
way as bay leaves are used in Western dishes. They are
available from supermarkets and Indian stores, as too are
ready-made curry pastes. These pastes may be mild or hot.*

EASY CHINESE CHICKEN

This is simplicity itself, requiring very little preparation, yet it is packed with flavour and makes a great midweek supper.

🍽 Serves 4

🥄 Preparation time: 10 minutes, plus 5 minutes' pre-cooking

🥣 Cooking time: 4 hours

Ingredients

2 tsp grated fresh root ginger

4 garlic cloves, finely chopped

2 star anise

150 ml/5 fl oz Chinese rice wine or
medium dry sherry

2 tbsp dark soy sauce

1 tsp sesame oil

4 skinless chicken thighs or drumsticks

shredded spring onions, to garnish

1 Mix together the ginger, garlic, star anise, rice wine, soy sauce and sesame oil in a bowl and stir in 5 tablespoons water. Place the chicken in a saucepan, add the spice mixture and bring to the boil.

2 Transfer to the slow cooker, cover and cook on low for 4 hours, or until the chicken is tender and cooked through.

3 Remove and discard the star anise. Transfer the chicken to warm plates and serve garnished with shredded spring onions.

Cook's tip
*Serve the chicken with plain boiled rice or egg noodles.
However, remember that brown rice contains about five
times as much fat as white rice.*

CHICKEN BRAISED WITH RED CABBAGE

This is a classic Northern European combination that is traditionally served in the winter when red cabbage is in season.

🍽 Serves 4

🥣 Preparation time: 15 minutes, plus 10 minutes' pre-cooking

🕐 Cooking time: 5 hours

Ingredients

2 tbsp sunflower oil

4 skinless chicken thighs or drumsticks

1 onion, chopped

500 g/1 lb 2 oz red cabbage, cored and shredded

2 apples, peeled and chopped

12 canned or cooked chestnuts, halved (optional)

½ tsp juniper berries

125 ml/4 fl oz red wine

salt and pepper

fresh flat-leaf parsley sprigs, to garnish

1 Heat the oil in a large, heavy-based saucepan. Add the chicken and cook, turning frequently, for 5 minutes until golden on all sides. Using a slotted spoon transfer to a plate lined with kitchen paper.

2 Add the onion to the saucepan and cook over a medium heat, stirring occasionally, until softened. Stir in the cabbage and apples and cook, stirring occasionally, for 5 minutes. Add the chestnuts, if using, juniper berries and wine and season to taste with salt and pepper. Bring to the boil.

3 Spoon half the cabbage mixture into the slow cooker, add the chicken pieces, then top with the remaining cabbage mixture. Cover and cook on low for 5 hours until the chicken is tender and cooked through. Serve immediately, garnished with sprigs of parsley.

Cook's tip
If possible, stir the mixture about halfway through the cooking time to ensure that all the cabbage is cooked through. Replace the lid as soon as possible afterwards – and use oven gloves if the lid is hot.

CHIPOTLE CHICKEN

Chipotle chillies are smoked jalapeños and they impart a distinctive flavour to this dish, but remember that they are still hot.

Serves 4

Preparation time: 10 minutes, plus 30 minutes' soaking, plus 5–10 minutes to finish

Cooking time: 5 hours

Ingredients

4–6 chipotle chillies

4 garlic cloves, unpeeled

1 small onion, chopped

400 g/14 oz canned chopped tomatoes

300 ml/10 fl oz hot chicken or
    vegetable stock

4 skinless chicken breast portions

salt and pepper

1 Preheat the oven to 200°C/400°F/Gas Mark 6. Place the chillies in a bowl and pour in just enough hot water to cover. Set aside to soak for 30 minutes. Meanwhile, place the unpeeled garlic cloves on a baking sheet and roast in the oven for about 10 minutes until soft. Remove from the oven and set aside to cool.

2 Drain the chillies, reserving 125 ml/4 fl oz of the soaking water. Deseed the chillies, if you like, and chop coarsely. Place the chillies and reserved soaking water in a blender or food processor and process to a purée. Peel and mash the garlic in a bowl.

3 Place the chilli purée, garlic, onion and tomatoes in the slow cooker and stir in the stock. Season the chicken portions with salt and pepper and place them in the slow cooker. Cover and cook on low for about 5 hours until the chicken is tender and cooked through.

4 Lift the chicken out of the slow cooker with a slotted spoon, cover and keep warm. Pour the cooking liquid into a saucepan and bring to the boil on the hob. Boil for 5–10 minutes until reduced. Place the chicken on warm plates, spoon the sauce over it and serve.

Cook's tip
Breast is the leanest chicken meat and, if you're on a low-fat diet, you should always make sure it is skinless as this reduces the fat content considerably.

Variation
If you want to save preparation time, used canned chipotle chillies in adobo sauce. These don't need to be soaked and you can simply purée them with the sauce.

CARIBBEAN BEEF STEW

*Packed with flavour and bursting with colour, this is a
perfect dish to come home to after a busy day.*

 Serves 6

Preparation time: 20 minutes, plus 10 minutes' pre-cooking

Cooking time: $7\frac{1}{2}$ hours

Ingredients

450 g/1 lb braising steak

450 g/1 lb diced pumpkin or other squash

1 onion, chopped

1 red pepper, deseeded and chopped

2 garlic cloves, finely chopped

2.5-cm/1-inch piece fresh root ginger,
  finely chopped

1 tbsp sweet or hot paprika

225 ml/8 fl oz beef stock

400 g/14 oz canned chopped tomatoes

400g/14 oz canned pigeon peas,
  drained and rinsed

400 g/14 oz canned black-eyed beans,
  drained and rinsed

salt and pepper

1 Trim off any visible fat from the steak, then dice the meat. Heat a large, heavy-based saucepan without
adding any extra fat. Add the meat and cook, stirring constantly, for a few minutes until golden all over.
Stir in the pumpkin, onion and red pepper and cook for 1 minute, then add the spices, stock and
tomatoes and bring to the boil.

2 Transfer the mixture to the slow cooker, cover and cook on low for 7 hours. Add the pigeon peas and
black-eyed beans to the stew and season to taste with salt and pepper. Re-cover and cook on high for
30 minutes, then serve.

Cook's tip
*Pigeon peas are also known as gunga peas, Jamaica
peas and Congo peas. Light brown in colour with darker
flecks, they are popular throughout the Caribbean. If you
can't find them, substitute canned chickpeas.*

MIXED BEAN CHILLI

This colourful dish makes an economical and tasty mid-week supper when served with boiled rice.

◎ Serves 4–6

☕ Preparation time: 10 minutes, plus overnight soaking, plus 25 minutes' pre-cooking

♨ Cooking time: 10 hours

Ingredients

2 tbsp corn oil

1 onion, chopped

1 garlic clove, finely chopped

1 fresh red chilli, deseeded and chopped

1 yellow pepper, deseeded and chopped

1 tsp ground cumin

1 tbsp chilli powder

115 g/4 oz dried red kidney beans, soaked overnight, drained and rinsed

115 g/4 oz dried black beans, soaked overnight, drained and rinsed

115 g/4 oz dried pinto beans, soaked overnight, drained and rinsed

1 litre/1¾ pints vegetable stock

1 tbsp sugar

salt and pepper

chopped fresh coriander, to garnish

1 Heat the oil in a large, heavy-based saucepan. Add the onion, garlic, chilli and yellow pepper and cook over a medium heat, stirring occasionally, for 5 minutes. Stir in the cumin and chilli powder and cook, stirring, for 1–2 minutes. Add the drained beans and stock and bring to the boil. Boil vigorously for 15 minutes.

2 Transfer the mixture to the slow cooker, cover and cook on low for 10 hours until the beans are tender.

3 Season the mixture with salt and pepper, then ladle about one-third into a bowl. Mash well with a potato masher, then return the mashed beans to the cooker and stir in the sugar. Serve immediately, sprinkled with chopped fresh coriander.

Cook's tip

Both kidney beans and black beans contain a toxin (pinto beans don't) that is destroyed by vigorous boiling. It is important, therefore, that they are precooked before being transferred to the slow cooker.

Variation

You can serve the beans sprinkled with diced, reduced-fat cheese. Use about 115 g/4 oz in total.

WINTER VEGETABLE MEDLEY

This makes a great vegetarian main course, but also goes well with lean roast meat, such as chicken.

Serves 4

Preparation time: 15 minutes, plus 10 minutes' pre-cooking

Cooking time: 3 hours

Ingredients

2 tbsp sunflower oil

2 onions, peeled and chopped

3 carrots, chopped

3 parsnips, chopped

2 bunches celery, chopped, leaves reserved

2 tbsp chopped fresh parsley

1 tbsp chopped fresh coriander

300 ml/10 fl oz vegetable stock

salt and pepper

1 Heat the oil in a large, heavy-based saucepan. Add the onions and cook over a medium heat, stirring occasionally, for 5 minutes until softened. Add the carrots, parsnips and celery and cook, stirring occasionally, for a further 5 minutes. Stir in the herbs, season with salt and pepper and pour in the stock. Bring to the boil.

2 Transfer the vegetable mixture to the slow cooker, cover and cook on high for 3 hours until tender. Taste and adjust the seasoning if necessary. Using a slotted spoon, transfer the medley to warm plates, then spoon over a little of the cooking liquid. Garnish with a few of the reserved celery leaves.

Cook's tip
Strain any leftover cooking liquid and store in the refrigerator or freezer to use as vegetable stock.

Variation
For a more substantial dish – with a slightly higher fat content – sprinkle thinly shaved Parmesan cheese over each portion or drizzle with 2 tablespoons double cream.

CHAPTER 4: EASY ENTERTAINING

BULGARIAN CHICKEN

East meets West in Bulgarian cuisine, as typified by the combination
of sweet paprika and hot chilli in this classic dish.

Serves 6

Preparation time: 20 minutes, plus 10 minutes' pre-cooking

Cooking time: 6 hours

Ingredients

4 tbsp sunflower oil

6 chicken portions

2 onions, chopped

2 garlic cloves, finely chopped

1 fresh red chilli, deseeded and finely chopped

6 tomatoes, peeled and chopped

2 tsp sweet paprika

1 bay leaf

225 ml/8 fl oz hot chicken stock

salt and pepper

fresh thyme sprigs, to garnish

1 Heat half the oil in a large, heavy-based frying pan. Add the chicken portions and cook over a medium heat, turning occasionally, for about 10 minutes, until golden all over.

2 Transfer the contents of the pan to the slow cooker and add the onions, garlic, chilli and tomatoes. Sprinkle in the paprika, add the bay leaf and pour in the stock. Season with salt and pepper. Stir well, cover and cook on low for 6 hours until the chicken is cooked through and tender. Serve immediately, garnished with sprigs of thyme.

Cook's tip
The cooking time can vary depending on the size
and type of the chicken portions. Test that the chicken
is cooked through by piercing the thickest part with
the point of a sharp knife. If the juices run clear,
with no hint of pink, the chicken is cooked.

CHICKEN CACCIATORE

Serve this traditional Italian dish with a crisp mixed salad rather than pasta if you are following a low-carb diet.

Serves 4

Preparation time: 20 minutes, plus 15 minutes' pre-cooking

Cooking time: 5 hours

Ingredients

3 tbsp olive oil

4 chicken portions, skinned

2 onions, sliced

2 garlic cloves, finely chopped

400 g/14 oz canned chopped tomatoes

1 tbsp tomato purée

2 tbsp chopped fresh parsley

2 tsp fresh thyme leaves

150 ml/5 fl oz red wine

salt and pepper

fresh thyme sprigs, to garnish

1 Heat the oil in a heavy-based frying pan. Add the chicken portions and cook over a medium heat, turning occasionally, for 10 minutes until golden all over. Using a slotted spoon, transfer the chicken to the slow cooker.

2 Add the onions to the pan and cook, stirring occasionally, for 5 minutes until softened and just turning golden. Add the garlic, tomatoes and their can juices, tomato purée, parsley, thyme and wine. Season with salt and pepper and bring to the boil.

3 Pour the tomato mixture over the chicken pieces. Cover and cook on low for 5 hours until the chicken is tender and cooked through. Taste and adjust the seasoning if necessary and serve, garnished with sprigs of thyme.

Cook's tip
Removing the skin from chicken before cooking it reduces the fat content considerably.

Variation
You can also make this dish with turkey legs, thighs or supremes, all of which become flavourful and juicy when cooked in this way.

LAMB SHANKS WITH OLIVES

This is the perfect choice for slow cooking as the meat becomes melt-in-the-mouth tender and the flavours mingle superbly.

Serves 4

Preparation time: 15 minutes, plus 15 minutes' pre-cooking

Cooking time: 8½ hours

Ingredients

1½ tbsp plain flour	2 tsp sugar
4 lamb shanks	225 ml/8 fl oz red wine
2 tbsp olive oil	5-cm/2-inch cinnamon stick
1 onion, sliced	2 fresh rosemary sprigs
2 garlic cloves, finely chopped	115 g/4 oz stoned black olives
2 tsp sweet paprika	2 tbsp lemon juice
400 g/14 oz canned chopped tomatoes	2 tbsp chopped fresh mint
2 tbsp tomato purée	salt and pepper
2 carrots, sliced	fresh mint sprigs, to garnish

1 Spread out the flour on a plate and season with salt and pepper. Toss the lamb in the seasoned flour and shake off any excess. Heat the oil in a large, heavy-based saucepan. Add the lamb shanks and cook over a medium heat, turning frequently, for 6–8 minutes until browned all over. Transfer to a plate and set aside.

2 Add the onions and garlic to the saucepan and cook, stirring frequently, for 5 minutes until softened. Stir in the paprika and cook for 1 minute. Add the tomatoes, tomato purée, carrots, sugar, wine, cinnamon stick and rosemary and bring to the boil.

3 Transfer the vegetable mixture to the slow cooker and add the lamb shanks. Cover and cook on low for 8 hours until the lamb is very tender.

4 Add the olives, lemon juice and mint to the slow cooker. Re-cover and cook on high for 30 minutes. Remove and discard the rosemary and cinnamon and serve, garnished with mint sprigs.

Cook's tip
Lamb shanks are quite unwieldy things. Most medium-sized slow cookers, especially oval ones, can handle four, but if you're planning to cook for more people, check in advance that you have sufficient room.

Variation
You could substitute 700 g/1 lb 9 oz boneless shoulder of lamb for the lamb shanks. Trim off any excess fat and cut the meat into 5-cm/2-inch cubes, then proceed as in the recipe.

Springtime Lamb with Asparagus

*Seasonal ingredients have a deliciously fresh flavour, but you can enjoy the
taste of springtime at any time of year if you use frozen asparagus.*

⦿| Serves 4

Preparation time: 20 minutes, plus 10 minutes' pre-cooking, plus 5 minutes to finish

Cooking time: 7¼ hours

Ingredients

2 tbsp sunflower oil

1 onion, thinly sliced

2 garlic cloves, very finely chopped

1 kg/2 lb 4 oz boneless shoulder of lamb,
   cut into 2.5-cm/1-in cubes

225 g/8 oz asparagus spears, thawed if frozen

300 ml/10 fl oz chicken stock

4 tbsp lemon juice

150 ml/5 fl oz double cream

salt and pepper

1 Heat the oil in a large, heavy-based frying pan. Add the onion and cook over a medium heat, stirring occasionally, for 5 minutes until softened. Add the garlic and lamb and cook, stirring occasionally, for a further 5 minutes until the lamb is lightly browned all over.

2 Meanwhile, trim off and reserve the tips of the asparagus spears. Cut the stalks into 2–3 pieces. Add the stock and lemon juice to the frying pan, season with salt and pepper and bring to the boil. Lower the heat, add the asparagus stalks and simmer for 2 minutes.

3 Transfer the mixture to the slow cooker. Cover and cook on low for 7 hours until the lamb is tender.

4 About 20 minutes before you intend to serve, cook the reserved asparagus tips in a saucepan of lightly salted boiling water for 5 minutes. Drain well, then mix with the cream. Spoon the cream mixture on top of the lamb mixture but do not stir it in. Re-cover and cook on high for 15–20 minutes to heat through before serving.

Cook's tip
*Lamb, particularly shoulder, is often quite fatty. Trim
off as much fat as possible before dicing the meat to
prevent a layer of grease from forming on top of the
stew. If it does, spoon off as much as possible before
adding the cream and asparagus mixture.*

Variation
*This dish also works well with veal with the bonus that
stewing veal is usually inexpensive. It is a fairly lean meat
with a special affinity with lemons and a delicate flavour
that will be complemented by the asparagus cream sauce.*

LAMB TAGINE

This North African combination of lamb, dried fruit and nuts is delicately spiced and wonderfully rich in flavour.

Serves 6

Preparation time: 15 minutes, plus 10 minutes' pre-cooking

Cooking time: 8 ½ hours

Ingredients

3 tbsp olive oil

2 red onions, chopped

2 garlic cloves, finely chopped

2.5-cm/1-inch piece fresh root ginger,
   finely chopped

1 yellow pepper, deseeded and chopped

1 kg/2 lb 4 oz boneless shoulder of lamb,
   trimmed and cut into 2.5-cm/1-inch cubes

850 ml/1 ½ pints lamb or chicken stock

225 g/8 oz ready-to-eat dried apricots, halved

1 tbsp clear honey

4 tbsp lemon juice

pinch of saffron threads

5-cm/2-inch cinnamon stick

salt and pepper

To garnish

55 g/2 oz flaked almonds, toasted

fresh coriander sprigs

1 Heat the oil in a large, heavy-based saucepan. Add the onions, garlic, ginger and yellow pepper and cook over a low heat, stirring occasionally, for 5 minutes until the onion has softened. Add the lamb and stir well to mix, then pour in the stock. Add the apricots, honey, lemon juice, saffron and cinnamon stick and season with the salt and pepper. Bring to the boil.

2 Transfer the mixture to the slow cooker. Cover and cook on low for 8 ½ hours until the meat is tender.

3 Remove and discard the cinnamon stick. Transfer to warm serving plates, sprinkle with the almonds, garnish with fresh coriander and serve.

JAMBALAYA

This Louisiana classic is thought to get its name from the French jambon or the Spanish jamón – meaning ham, which is a traditional ingredient.

 Serves 6

 Preparation time: 20 minutes, plus 15 minutes' pre-cooking

 Cooking time: 6½ hours

Ingredients

½ tsp cayenne pepper

½ tsp freshly ground black pepper

1 tsp salt

2 tsp chopped fresh thyme

350 g/12 oz skinless, boneless chicken
   breasts, diced

2 tbsp corn oil

2 onions, chopped

2 garlic cloves, finely chopped

2 green peppers, deseeded and chopped

2 celery sticks, chopped

115 g/4 oz smoked ham, chopped

175 g/6 oz chorizo sausage, sliced

400 g/14 oz canned chopped tomatoes

2 tbsp tomato purée

225 ml/8 fl oz chicken stock

450 g/1 lb peeled raw prawns

450 g/1 lb cooked rice

snipped fresh chives, to garnish

1 Mix together the cayenne, black pepper, salt and thyme in a bowl. Add the chicken and toss to coat. Heat the oil in a large, heavy-based saucepan. Add the onions, garlic, green peppers and celery and cook over a low heat, stirring occasionally, for 5 minutes. Add the chicken and cook over a medium heat, stirring frequently, for a further 5 minutes until golden all over. Stir in the ham, chorizo, tomatoes, tomato purée and stock and bring to the boil.

2 Transfer the mixture to the slow cooker. Cover and cook on low for 6 hours. Add the prawns and rice, re-cover and cook on high for 30 minutes.

3 Taste and adjust the seasoning, if necessary. Transfer to warm plates, garnish with chives and serve the jambalaya immediately.

Cook's tip
Traditional recipes add raw rice towards the end of the cooking time. Using cooked rice makes this rather less hit-and-miss. Alternatively, just add the prawns in step 2 and simply serve the jambalaya on a bed of freshly cooked rice.

BOEUF BOURGUIGNONNE

*It is well worth buying a full-bodied, good-quality red wine –
preferably Burgundy – for this perennially popular French classic.*

◎ Serves 6
Preparation time: 15 minutes, plus 15 minutes' pre-cooking
Cooking time: 7¼ hours

Ingredients

6 rashers streaky bacon, derinded and chopped

2 tbsp plain flour

900 g/2 lb braising steak, trimmed and cut into
   2.5-cm/1-inch cubes

3 tbsp olive oil

25 g/1 oz unsalted butter

12 baby onions or shallots

2 garlic cloves, finely chopped

150 ml/5 fl oz beef stock

450 ml/16 fl oz full-bodied red wine

bouquet garni

140 g/5 oz mushrooms, sliced

salt and pepper

1 Cook the bacon in a large, heavy-based saucepan, stirring occasionally, until the fat runs and the
pieces are crisp. Meanwhile, spread out the flour on a plate and season with salt and pepper. Toss the
steak cubes in the flour to coat, shaking off any excess. Using a slotted spoon, transfer the bacon to a
plate. Add the oil to the saucepan. When it is hot, add the steak cubes and cook, in batches, stirring
occasionally, for 5 minutes until browned all over. Transfer to the plate with a slotted spoon.

2 Add the butter to the saucepan. When it has melted, add the onions and garlic and cook, stirring
occasionally, for 5 minutes. Return the bacon and steak to the pan and pour in the stock and wine.
Bring to the boil.

3 Transfer the mixture to the slow cooker and add the bouquet garni. Cover and cook on low for
7 hours until the meat is tender.

4 Add the mushrooms to the slow cooker and stir well. Re-cover and cook on high for 15 minutes.

5 Remove and discard the bouquet garni. Adjust the seasoning if necessary, then serve immediately.

Cook's tip
*Boeuf bourguignonne is even better served the next
day. Leave to cool, then transfer to a suitable container
and store in the refrigerator. Skim off any fat from the
surface and reheat in a large saucepan set over a
low heat. Never reheat food in the slow cooker.*

Variation
*If the sauce looks too thin, add 1–2 tablespoons cornflour
mixed to a paste with a little water when you add the
mushrooms. Stir it in well before replacing the lid.*

DUCKLING WITH APPLES

As the duckling is braised gently, all the meat becomes deliciously
tender, so you can use the whole bird for this tasty French dish.

Serves 4

Preparation time: 15 minutes, plus 15 minutes' pre-cooking, plus 5 minutes to finish

Cooking time: 8 hours

Ingredients

1.8–2 kg/4–4 lb 8 oz duckling, cut into 8 pieces	300 ml/10 fl oz dry white wine
2 tbsp olive oil	bouquet garni
1 onion, finely chopped	55 g/2 oz unsalted butter
1 carrot, finely chopped	4 eating apples
300 ml/10 fl oz chicken stock	salt and pepper

1 Season the duckling pieces with salt and pepper. Heat the oil in a large, heavy-based frying pan. Add all the duckling pieces, placing the breast portions skin side down. Cook over a medium-high heat for a few minutes until golden brown, then transfer the breast portions to a plate. Turn the other pieces and continue to cook until browned all over. Transfer to the plate.

2 Add the onion and carrot to the frying pan and cook over a low heat, stirring occasionally, for 5 minutes until the onion is softened. Add the stock and wine and bring to the boil.

3 Transfer the vegetable mixture to the slow cooker. Add the duckling pieces and the bouquet garni. Cover and cook on low for 8 hours, occasionally skimming off the fat from the slow cooker and replacing the lid immediately each time.

4 Shortly before you are ready to serve, peel, core and slice the apples. Melt the butter in a large frying pan. Add the apple slices and cook over a medium heat, turning occasionally, for 5 minutes until golden.

5 Spoon the cooked apples onto warm plates and divide the duckling among them. Skim off the fat and strain the sauce into a jug, then pour it over the duckling and serve.

Cook's tip
Ready-made bouquets garnis, either resembling tea bags
or tied in a square of muslin, are available from
supermarkets. If you want to use fresh herbs, tie together
3 parsley sprigs, 1 thyme sprig and 1–2 bay leaves.

Neapolitan Beef

Most regions of Italy boast of their stufato – slow-braised beef – and, hardly surprisingly, in Naples the recipe includes tomatoes.

Serves 6

Preparation time: 15 minutes, plus 12 hours' marinating, plus 15 minutes' pre-cooking

Cooking time: 9 hours

Ingredients

300 ml/10 fl oz red wine

4 tbsp olive oil

1 celery stick, chopped

2 shallots, sliced

4 garlic cloves, finely chopped

1 bay leaf

10 fresh basil leaves

3 fresh parsley sprigs

pinch of grated nutmeg

pinch of ground cinnamon

2 cloves

1.5 kg/3 lb 5 oz beef

silverside

1–2 garlic cloves, thinly sliced

55 g/2 oz streaky bacon or

pancetta, derinded and

chopped

400g/14 oz canned chopped

tomatoes

2 tbsp tomato purée

salt and pepper

1 Combine the wine, 2 tablespoons of the olive oil, the celery, shallots, garlic, herbs and spices in a large, non-metallic bowl. Add the beef, cover and marinate, turning occasionally, for 12 hours.

2 Drain the beef, reserving the marinade, and pat dry with kitchen paper. Make small incisions all over the beef using a sharp knife. Insert a slice of garlic and a piece of bacon in each 'pocket'. Heat the remaining oil in a large frying pan. Add the meat and cook over a medium heat, turning frequently, until browned all over. Transfer to the slow cooker.

3 Strain the reserved marinade into the frying pan and bring to the boil. Stir in the tomatoes and tomato purée. Stir well, then pour the mixture over the beef. Cover and cook on low for about 9 hours until tender. If possible, turn the beef over halfway through the cooking time.

4 To serve, remove the beef and place on a carving board. Cover with foil and leave to stand for 10–15 minutes to firm up. Cut into slices and transfer to a platter. Spoon over the sauce and serve immediately.

SWEET-AND-SOUR SICILIAN PASTA

This colourful vegetarian sauce is a little like the classic French dish ratatouille but has an extra tang of balsamic vinegar and lemon juice.

Serves 4

Preparation time: 15 minutes, plus 15 minutes' pre-cooking

Cooking time: 5 hours

Ingredients

4 tbsp olive oil

1 large red onion, sliced

2 garlic cloves, finely chopped

2 red peppers, deseeded and sliced

2 courgettes, cut into batons

1 aubergine, cut into batons

450 ml/16 fl oz passata

4 tbsp lemon juice

2 tbsp balsamic vinegar

55 g/2 oz stoned black olives, sliced

1 tbsp sugar

400 g/14 oz dried fettuccine

salt and pepper

fresh flat-leaf parsley sprigs, to garnish

1 Heat the oil in a large, heavy-based saucepan. Add the onion, garlic and peppers and cook over a low heat, stirring occasionally, for 5 minutes. Add the courgettes and aubergine and cook, stirring occasionally, for 5 minutes more. Stir in the passata and 150 ml/5 fl oz water and bring to the boil. Stir in the lemon juice, vinegar, olives and sugar and season with salt and pepper.

2 Transfer the mixture to the slow cooker. Cover and cook on low for 5 hours until all the vegetables are tender.

3 To cook the pasta, bring a large saucepan of lightly salted water to the boil. Add the fettuccine and bring back to the boil. Cook for 10–12 minutes until the pasta is tender but still firm to the bite. Drain and transfer to a warm serving dish. Spoon the vegetable mixture over the pasta, toss lightly, garnish with parsley and serve.

Cook's tip
When cooking any type of pasta, make sure that the water is boiling, not merely simmering. This prevents the ribbons or strands from sticking together.

BOUILLABAISSE

This is only one, although perhaps the most famous, of Mediterranean fish soups. For the best flavour, it should include a variety of different fish.

Serves 6

Preparation time: 45 minutes

Cooking time: 8 1/2 hours

Ingredients

2.25 kg/5 lb mixed white fish, such as
    red mullet, sea bream, sea bass, monkfish
    and whiting, filleted and bones and heads
    reserved, if possible

450 g/1 lb raw prawns

grated rind of 1 orange

pinch of saffron threads

4 garlic cloves, finely chopped

225 ml/8 fl oz olive oil

2 onions, finely chopped

1 leek, thinly sliced

4 potatoes, thinly sliced

2 large tomatoes, peeled and chopped

1 bunch fresh flat-leaf parsley, chopped

1 fresh fennel sprig

1 fresh thyme sprig

1 bay leaf

2 cloves

6 black peppercorns

1 strip orange rind

sea salt

crusty bread or croûtes, to serve

1 Cut the fish fillets into bite-sized pieces and peel and devein the prawns. Reserve the heads and shells of the prawns. Rinse the fish bones, if using, and cut off the gills of any fish heads. Place the chunks of fish and the prawns in a large bowl. Sprinkle with the grated orange rind, saffron, half the garlic and 2 tablespoons of the oil. Cover and set aside in the refrigerator.

2 Put the remaining garlic, the onions, leek, potatoes, tomatoes, parsley, fennel, thyme, bay leaf, cloves, peppercorns and strip of orange rind in the slow cooker. Add the fish heads and bones, if using, and the prawn shells and heads. Pour in the remaining olive oil and 2.8 litres/5 pints boiling water or enough to cover the ingredients by 2.5 cm/1 inch. Season with sea salt. Cover and cook on low for 8 hours.

3 Strain the stock and return the liquid to the slow cooker. Discard the flavourings, fish and prawn trimmings but retain the vegetables and return them to the slow cooker if you like. Add the fish and prawn mixture, re-cover and cook on high for 30 minutes until the fish is cooked through and flakes easily with the point of a knife.

4 Ladle into warm bowls and serve with crusty bread or croûtes.

Moroccan Sea Bream

Delicate North African spices complement the delicious flavour
of this attractive fish which is usually cooked whole.

◎ Serves 2

🥣 Preparation time: 15 minutes, plus 10 minutes' pre-cooking, plus 5 minutes to finish

🕒 Cooking time: 6½–6¾ hours

Ingredients

2 tbsp olive oil

2 onions, chopped

2 garlic cloves, finely chopped

2 carrots, finely chopped

1 fennel bulb, finely chopped

½ tsp ground cumin

½ tsp ground cloves

1 tsp ground coriander

pinch of saffron threads

300 ml/10 fl oz fish stock

1 preserved or fresh lemon

900 g/2 lb sea bream, cleaned

salt and pepper

1 Heat the oil in a large, heavy-based saucepan. Add the onions, garlic, carrots and fennel and cook over a medium heat, stirring occasionally, for 5 minutes. Stir in all the spices and cook, stirring, for a further 2 minutes. Pour in the stock, season with salt and pepper and bring to the boil.

2 Transfer the mixture to the slow cooker. Cover and cook on low for 6 hours or until the vegetables are tender.

3 Rinse the preserved lemon if using. Discard the fish head if you like. Slice the lemon and place the slices in the fish cavity, then place the fish in the slow cooker. Re-cover and cook on high for 30–45 minutes until the flesh flakes easily with the point of a knife.

4 Carefully transfer the fish to a platter and spoon the vegetables around it. Cover and keep warm. Transfer the cooking liquid to a saucepan and boil for a few minutes until reduced. Spoon it over the fish and serve.

Cook's tip
This recipe also works extremely well with sea bass.
Before cooking, cut off the sharply spined fins.

CABBAGE ROULADES WITH TOMATO SAUCE

These tasty stuffed cabbage rolls make a great vegetarian main course but can also be served as a starter, in which case make half the quantity.

Serves 6

Preparation time: 25 minutes, plus 20 minutes' pre-cooking

Cooking time: 3–4 hours

Ingredients

225 g/8 oz mixed nuts, finely ground

2 onions, finely chopped

1 garlic clove, finely chopped

2 celery sticks, finely chopped

115 g/4 oz Cheddar cheese, grated

1 tsp finely chopped thyme

2 eggs

1 tsp yeast extract

12 large green cabbage leaves

Tomato sauce

2 tbsp sunflower oil

2 onions, chopped

2 garlic cloves, finely chopped

600 g/1 lb 5 oz canned
   chopped tomatoes

2 tbsp tomato purée

1 1/2 tsp sugar

1 bay leaf

salt and pepper

1 First make the tomato sauce. Heat the oil in a heavy-based saucepan. Add the onion and cook over a medium heat, stirring occasionally, for 5 minutes until softened. Stir in the garlic and cook for 1 minute, then add the tomatoes, tomato purée, sugar and bay leaf. Season with salt and pepper and bring to the boil. Lower the heat and simmer gently for 20 minutes until thickened.

2 Meanwhile, mix together the nuts, onions, garlic, celery, cheese and thyme in a bowl. Lightly beat the eggs with the yeast extract in a jug, then stir into the nut mixture. Set aside.

3 Cut out the thick stalk from the cabbage leaves. Blanch the leaves in a large saucepan of boiling water for 5 minutes, then drain and refresh under cold water. Pat dry with kitchen paper.

4 Place a little of the nut mixture on the stalk end of each cabbage leaf. Fold the sides over, then roll up to make a neat parcel.

5 Arrange the parcels in the slow cooker, seam side down. Remove and discard the bay leaf from the tomato sauce and pour the sauce over the cabbage rolls. Cover and cook on low for 3–4 hours. Serve the cabbage roulades hot or cold.

AUBERGINE TIMBALES

Served with a quick and easy sauce and a salad, these attractive moulds make an unusual vegetarian main course.

🍽 Serves 4

🥣 Preparation time: 15 minutes, plus 20–25 minutes' pre-cooking

🕙 Cooking time: 2 hours

Ingredients

2 aubergines

3 tbsp olive oil, plus extra for greasing

2 onions, finely chopped

2 red peppers, deseeded and chopped

1 large tomato, peeled and chopped

6 tbsp milk

2 egg yolks

pinch of ground cinnamon

85 g/3 oz crispbread, finely crushed

salt and pepper

fresh coriander sprigs, to garnish

For the sauce

300 ml/10 fl oz soured cream

3–4 tbsp sun-dried tomato paste (optional)

1 Halve the aubergines and scoop out the flesh with a spoon. Reserve the shells and dice the flesh. Heat the oil in a large, heavy-based frying pan. Add the onions and cook over a low heat, stirring occasionally, for 5 minutes. Add the diced aubergines, red peppers and tomato and cook, stirring occasionally, for 15–20 minutes, until all the vegetables are soft. Remove the pan from the heat.

2 Transfer the mixture to a food processor or blender and process to a purée, then scrape into a bowl. Beat together the milk, egg yolks, cinnamon and salt and pepper in a jug, then stir into the vegetable purée.

3 Brush 4 ramekins or cups with oil and sprinkle with the crispbread crumbs to coat. Tip out any excess. Mix about three-quarters of the remaining crumbs into the vegetable purée. Slice the aubergine shells into strips and use them to line the ramekins, leaving the ends protruding above the rims. Spoon the filling into the ramekins, sprinkle with the remaining crumbs and fold the overlapping ends over.

4 Cover with foil and place in the slow cooker. Pour in sufficient boiling water to come about one-third of the way up the sides of the ramekins. Cover and cook on high for 2 hours.

5 To make the sauce, lightly beat the soured cream and add the tomato paste to taste, if desired. Season with salt and pepper. Lift the ramekins out of the cooker and remove the foil. Invert onto serving plates and serve with the sauce, garnished with coriander sprigs.

CHAPTER 5: DESSERTS

Magic Lemon Sponge

This deliciously tangy dessert is a good, old-fashioned family favourite
that looks and smells tempting and tastes scrumptious.

🍽 Serves 4
🥄 Preparation time: 20 minutes
🧤 Cooking time: 2½ hours

Ingredients

140 g/5 oz caster sugar
3 eggs, separated
300 ml/10 fl oz milk
3 tbsp self-raising flour, sifted
150 ml/5 fl oz freshly squeezed lemon juice
icing sugar, for dusting

1 Beat the sugar with the egg yolks in a bowl, using an electric mixer. Gradually beat in the milk, followed by the flour and the lemon juice.

2 Whisk the egg whites in a separate, grease-free bowl until stiff. Fold half the whites into the yolk mixture using a rubber or plastic spatula in a figure-of-eight movement, then fold in the remainder. Try not to knock out the air.

3 Pour the mixture into an ovenproof dish, cover with foil and place in the slow cooker. Add sufficient boiling water to come about one-third of the way up the side of the dish. Cover and cook on high for 2½ hours until the mixture has set and the sauce and sponge have separated.

4 Lift the dish out of the cooker and discard the foil. Lightly sift a little icing sugar over the top and serve.

Cook's tip
Don't worry if the mixture looks as if it is slightly curdled
after you have folded in the egg whites. It will be all right.

APPLE CRUMBLE

*Served hot or cold, on its own or accompanied by cream, custard
or ice cream, this is always a sure-fire family favourite.*

🍽 Serves 4

🥄 Preparation time: 15 minutes

🧤 Cooking time: 5½ hours

Ingredients

55 g/2 oz plain flour

55 g/2 oz rolled oats

150 g/5½ oz light muscovado sugar

½ tsp grated nutmeg

½ tsp ground cinnamon

115 g/4 oz butter, softened

4 cooking apples, peeled, cored and sliced

4–5 tbsp apple juice

1 Sift the flour into a bowl and stir in the oats, sugar, nutmeg and cinnamon. Add the butter and mix in with a pastry blender or the prongs of a fork.

2 Place the apple slices in the base of the slow cooker and add the apple juice. Sprinkle the flour mixture evenly over them.

3 Cover and cook on low for 5½ hours. Serve hot, warm or cold.

Cook's tip
*Ground nutmeg loses its aroma and flavour very
quickly. It is better to buy whole nutmegs and
grate them freshly just before using.*

Variation
*Sprinkle 115 g/4 oz mixed dried fruit over the apple
slices before adding the crumble topping.*

Thai Black Rice Pudding

Glutinous or sticky rice is very popular in Thailand. The black variety has an unusual, nutty flavour and looks intriguing.

🍽 Serves 4

🥄 Preparation time: 5 minutes, plus 15 minutes' pre-cooking

🧤 Cooking time: 2–2½ hours

Ingredients

175 g/6 oz black glutinous rice

2 tbsp light brown sugar

450 ml/16 fl oz canned coconut milk

3 eggs

2 tbsp caster sugar

1 Mix together the rice, brown sugar and half the coconut milk in a saucepan, then stir in 225 ml/8 fl oz water. Bring to the boil, then reduce the heat and simmer, stirring occasionally, for 15 minutes until almost all the liquid has been absorbed. Transfer the mixture to a heatproof dish or individual ramekins.

2 Lightly beat the eggs with the remaining coconut milk and the caster sugar. Strain, then pour the mixture over the rice.

3 Cover with foil and place the dish in the slow cooker. Pour in enough boiling water to come about one-third of the way up the side of the dish. Cover and cook on high for 2–2½ hours until set. Remove the dish from the cooker and discard the foil before serving either hot or cold.

Cook's tip
Both black and white glutinous rice are available from many supermarkets and Asian food stores.

Variation
This dish is particularly refreshing and attractive if served with slices of fresh mango fanned out on the plates beside it.

BLUSHING PEARS

*This easy, yet very appealing dessert is great for dinner
parties but not really suitable for serving to children.*

🍽 Serves 6

🥣 Preparation time: 15 minutes, plus cooling and chilling

🖐 Cooking time: 4 hours

Ingredients

6 small ripe pears

225 ml/8 fl oz ruby port

200 g/7 oz caster sugar

1 tsp finely chopped crystallized ginger

2 tbsp lemon juice

whipped cream or Greek yogurt, to serve

1 Peel the pears, cut them in half lengthways and scoop out the cores. Place them in the slow cooker.

2 Mix together the port, sugar, ginger and lemon juice in a jug and pour the mixture over the pears.
Cover and cook on low for 4 hours until the pears are tender.

3 Leave the pears to cool in the slow cooker, then carefully transfer to a bowl and chill in the refrigerator
until required.

4 To serve, partially cut each pear half into about 6 slices lengthways, leaving the fruit intact at the stalk
end. Carefully lift the pear halves onto serving plates and press gently to fan out the slices. Serve with
whipped cream or yogurt.

Cook's tip
*The easiest way to scoop out the cores from the pear
halves is with a melon baller.*

Variation
*If you substitute medium white wine for the port, the dessert
won't be so colourful, but it will taste equally delicious.*

ITALIAN BREAD PUDDING

This is a sophisticated version of the popular pudding using panettone, a light-textured Italian Christmas cake flavoured with citrus rind and sultanas.

🍽 Serves 6

🥄 Preparation time: 20 minutes, plus cooling and chilling

🧤 Cooking time: 2½ hours

Ingredients

unsalted butter, for greasing

6 slices panettone

3 tbsp Marsala wine

300 ml/10 fl oz milk

300 ml/10 fl oz single cream

100 g/3½ oz caster sugar

grated rind of ½ lemon

pinch of ground cinnamon

3 large eggs, lightly beaten

double cream, to serve

1 Grease a pudding basin and set aside. Place the panettone on a deep plate and sprinkle with the Marsala wine.

2 Pour the milk and cream into a saucepan and add the sugar, lemon rind and cinnamon. Gradually bring to the boil over a low heat, stirring until the sugar has dissolved. Remove the pan from the heat and leave to cool slightly, then pour the mixture onto the eggs, beating constantly.

3 Place the panettone in the prepared dish, pour in the egg mixture and cover with foil. Place in the slow cooker and add enough boiling water to come about one-third of the way up the side of the dish. Cover and cook on high for 2½ hours until set.

4 Remove the dish from the slow cooker and discard the foil. Leave to cool, then chill in the refrigerator until required. Loosen the sides of the pudding and turn out onto a serving dish. Serve with cream on the side.

Cook's tip

A 1-litre/1¾-pint pudding basin gives the best shape for turning out, but if you don't have one, cook and serve the pudding in an ordinary ovenproof dish.

Variation

Panettone is widely available from supermarkets and Italian delicatessens, especially at Christmas time. However, if you can't find it, substitute slices of a light fruit loaf.

INDEX